FUNDAMENTALS
of
TIBETAN MEDICINE

ACCORDING TO THE *RGYUD-BZHI*

MEN-TSEE-KHANG
(Tibetan Medical & Astrological Institute of H.H. the Dalai Lama)

First Edition 1981
Second Revised Edition 1995
Third Edition 1997

FUNDAMENTALS OF TIBETAN MEDICINE

© Men-Tsee-Khang
(Tibetan Medical & Astrological Institute of H.H. the Dalai Lama)

(2000: 4/97)
ISBN: 81-86419-04-7

Cover art: Dr. D. Dawa, Men-Tsee-Khang
Artist: Lhaksam, Men-Tsee-Khang
Photo: Tenzin Dorjee, DIIR, CTA, Dharamsala

Published by Men-Tsee-Khang
Printed at Indraprastha Press (CBT),
Nehru House, New Delhi-110002

CONTENTS

Foreword
Preface to the Second Edition

PART ONE
CONCEPTS OF TRADITIONAL TIBETAN MEDICINE

PART TWO
ALLEGORICAL TREE

PART THREE

Notes
References
Transliteration
Contents of *rGyud-bzhi*
Bibliography

FOREWORD

The First Edition of the Fundamentals of Tibetan Medicine was well received. The Review Committee took meticulous efforts to bring out this revised edition, to coincide with a three month tour of eight European Countries in September, 1995, during which it will be distributed. I am sure the tour, consisting of exhibition and lectures on Tibetan medicine and astrology, will create a lot of interest in our ancient and unique system of healing. This book, therefore, intends to keep alive that interest, as well as, provide an authentic source for those who wish to learn more about the science and philosophy of Tibetan medicine.

Dr. Namgyal Qusar, Dr. Thokmay Paljor, Dr. Tenzin Dakpa and Dr. Lobsang Tsultrim have worked very hard to bring out this new edition, and suggestions have also been given by Dr. Pema Dorjee and Dr.Dorjee Rapten. For all of their efforts, I am deeply grateful.

The team who compiled the first edition had laid some excellent foundations for the work which was done on the second edition. However, there is a significant difference between the two teams, which is worth while mentioning. The first team was comprised of medical professionals who did not know English and, therefore, all their work had to be translated and explained to English speaking people, not trained in medicine. The team for the second edition, however, were all doctors with a good command of the English language and were able, thus, to work directly in this medium. In addition , they had all previously had good experiences in lecturing, clinical tasks, research and medical conferences. Also, because of the developments made in the study of Tibetan medicine since the publication of the first edition, the second team has not had many of the difficulties faced by their predecessors.

Mr. Gyaltsen Terkong, Deputy Director of our Documentation and Publication Department, has very professionally been responsible for the computer settings and other publication related tasks.

T. Tashi
Director

PREFACE TO THE SECOND EDITION

The First Edition of the Fundamentals of Tibetan Medicine was published to introduce the principles of an ancient system previously unwritten about to any great extent in the English languages. It was largely the creation of Prof. Drakton Jampa Gyaltsen, Dr. Lobsang Chophel, and Mr. Tsewang Jigme Tsarong who formed the editorial team. The book has remained one of the most popular and widely used publication on Tibetan medicine available in English.

Due to an increasingly interest in Tibetan medicine and a greater demand for literature on the subject, the need for the publication of an updated edition of this book was felt long time ago. It has finally been made possible under the directorship of Mr. Tsering Tashi, without whose initiative and encouragement, the project may still have taken a few more years to implement.

The responsibility for reviving the text in order to make it more comprehensive was given to a review committee. The second edition, whilst retaining more or less its original format, has been updated thoroughly. In particular, alterations, additions, and deletions have been made according to research and other reference materials on *rGyud-bzhi*, the only fundamental text of Tibetan medicine, and *Vaidurya sNgon-po*, the most popular commentary on this text, written by Desi Sangye Gyatso (1653-1705 A.D.). Some new photographs and illustrations have been also added to help its readers better understand some of the explanation.

We have endeavoured to our utmost to make this publication as authoritative as possible, but mistake may have appeared unknowingly, for which we hold full responsibility. Any useful intimations and suggestions which may help to improve the quality of the book are always welcome.

It is our hope that the second edition of this book will encourage a wider readership and facilitate a better understanding of Tibetan medicine amongst those who are interested. May those who read it lead a healthier and peaceful life.

Review Committee: Dr. Namgyal Qusar
Dr. Thokmay Paljor
Dr. Tenzin Dakpa
Dr. Lobsang Tsultrim

INTRODUCTION

Birth, old age, disease and death has always been part and parcel of our life in the realm of this cyclic existence. However, mankind always sought and devised theories to explain the causes of disease and developed various techniques for its prevention, alleviation, and cure. In each society, interpretations of health and disease differ from one to another, in accordance with their unique cultural backgrounds.

The primitive man ascribed disease to the evil influences of malignant souls (ghosts, devils etc.), magic, and incantations. The ancient Jews regarded disease as an expression of the wrath of God. The Chinese viewed disease as disharmony between two opposing forces of Yin and Yang or the Five Elements. The Indian Ayurvedists viewed disease as a result of improper proportion of the Tridoshas of Vayu, Pitta, and Kapha, while ancient Greek medicine attribute the causes of disease to the disharmony of phlegm, black bile, yellow bile and blood.

The understanding of health and disease in Tibetan society is explained extensively in a system of healing known as *gSo-ba Rig-pa* or the Science of Healing. The original teachings of this system are generally attributed to the Buddha who is said to have taught the root of this tradition in the manifestation of Medicine Buddha (Skt: Bhaishajya Guru; Tib: *Sangs-rgyas sMan-bla*). The essential aspects of his teachings are touched widely in the *rGyud-bzhi* or the Four Tantras.

THE *RGYUD-BZHI*

The complete Sanskrit title of this work is "Amrta Hrdya Astanga Guhyopadesa Tantra"[1]. The Tibetan title is : *"bDud-rtsi sNying-po Yan-lag brGyad-pa gSang-ba Man-ngag gi rGyud*[2]" or in English it could be translated as "The Secret Quintessential instructions on the Eight Branches of the Ambrosia Essence Tantra".

The *rGyud-bzhi* - Four Tantras

Some accounts say that original Sanskrit version of *rGud-bzhi* was probably written during the fourth century A.D.[3] and was translated into Tibetan by *Vairochana* and Kashmiri Pandit Chandrananda. They then gave *rGyud-bzh*i to King *Khri-srong lDe'u-btsan* (755-797 A.D.) and to the royal court

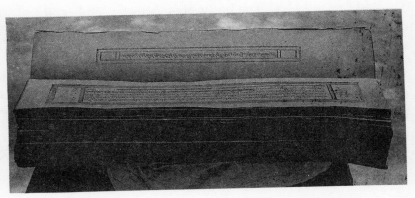

Vaidurya sNgon-po - the most popular commentary of the *rGyud-bzhi*, written by Desi Sangye Gyatso during 17th Century A.D.

physician, the Elder Yuthog Yontan Gonpo (708-833 A.D.)[4]. It is most likely that after the famous international medical conference at Samye, Tibet, Yuthog synthesised the best of the then known medical systems and rewrote the *rGyud-bzhi*.[5] This text was finally redacted by his most famous descendent, the Younger Yuthog Yontan Gonpo (1126-1202 A.D.) into the present version. He also wrote 18 other supplement works on *rGyud-bzhi*.[6]

The *rGyud-bzhi* was written in question and answer form between Rishi master *Rig-pa'i-Ye-Shes* and disciple Rishi *Yid-las-sKyes*, both of whom were emanations of the Medicine Buddha.[7] The work is divided into four independent texts containing 156 chapters with 5,900 verses - all of which deal with the following eight branches of medicine:

(1) *Lus*	The body (this includes embryology, anatomy, physiology, pathology, pharmacology, etc.)
(2) *Byis-pa*	Pediatrics
(3) *Mo-nad*	Gynaecology
(4) *gDon*	Disorders caused by evil spirits
(5) *mTshon*	Disorders of wounds inflicted by missile
(6) *Dug*	Toxicology
(7) *rGas*	Rejuvenation
(8) *Ro-Tsa*	Aphrodisiac.

AETIOLOGY OF *NYES-PA-GSUM*
AT PRIMORDIAL LEVEL

Opposed to the Cartisean view of life which reduces man to a mere machine, the Buddhist view holds that man *qua man* is a composite whole of mind, body and spirit. Hence, the Tibetan art of healing is an integrated or wholistic approach to health care. Disease, essentially means that there is a dynamic disequilibrium of various psychological and cosmo-physical elements that are caused at two different levels. At the primordial level, the aetiology of *Nyes-pa-gsum*[8] is explained by the psychical theory of *Dug-gsum*[9] and the cosmo-physical theory of *'Byung-ba lNga*. On the other hand, at a more immediate level, a disease is primarily caused by improper dietary, behavioural, seasonal and environmental factors.

The *Dug-gSum* Theory

Buddhist view holds that everything within the universe are in a constant state of flux: that all phenomena are charac-terised by impermanence and that the only permanent feature is its impermanence. "No matter whether perfect beings arise or not," the Buddha said, "it remains a fact and hard necessi-ty of existence that all creations are transitory."

It is this very impermanence of creation that causes each and every being, at one stage or another, to suffer. Suffering is not accidental but springs from a specific cause, whether from this life or from the previous lives. The extinction of suffering means the liberation from the vicious cycle of existence and this, is accomplished through the proper learning and gen-uine practice of the Dharma.

The Buddha traced the specific cause of all sufferings to the concept of *bDag-'dzin*[10] or Ego which is manifested in the form of *gTi-mug* (delusion, ignorance, confusion). This, in turn, give rise to *'Dod-chags* (attachment, greed, desire) and *Zhe-sdang* (hatred, aversion, aggression). In comparing these "three poisons" with a fire, which permanently consumes man, the Buddha said: "It burns through the fire of delusion, through the fire of attachment, through the fire of hatred, it burns through birth, old age, and death, through grief, lamentation, pain, sorrow and despair."

The "three mental poisons" of *'Dod-chags, Zhe-sdang* and *gTi-mug*, give rise to *rLung, mKhris-pa*, and *Bad-kan* disorders respectively. An in-depth study of the "three poisons" is found in Buddhist philosophy and psychology, and for our purpose, it is important to note the close interrelationship between mental and a physical disorder.

The *'Byung-ba lNga* Theory

This theory states that all phenomena, whether in the macrocosmic or in the microcosmic world, are formed by the five cosmo-physical elements of : (1) *Sa* (Earth); (2) *Chu* (Water); (3) *Me* (Fire); (4) *rLung* (Air); and *Nam-mkha* (Space). The body, being partly physical, is also composed of these five basic cosmo-physical elements. Hence, a disorder also involves a disequilibrium of these elements and their relationship is given in Table No. 1.

The five cosmo-physical elements are not the static physico-chemical elements, but dynamic forces which deal more with their inherent energetical function rather than their actual state. For instance, Water, does not mean a molecule of H_2O but its inherent energetical function to bring about a quality of heaviness, flexibility, coolness, etc.

TABLE 1

RELATIONSHIP BETWEEN THE AFFLICTIONS AND
THE FIVE COSMO-PHYSICAL ELEMENTS

Cosmo-Physical Elements	Affliction
Earth & Water	*Bad-kan*
Fire	*mKhris-pa*
Air	*rLung*

(Spatial Element is all pervasive)

Going beyond what is presently labelled as matter, these sub-atomic elements are applicable to both the macrocosmic as well as the microcosmic world as illustrated below:

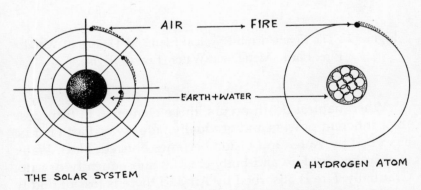

Figure 1: Application of Five Cosmo-Physical Elements to both the Microcosmic and the Macrocosmic world

Even though all the five cosmo-physical elements are responsible for the formation of a single tissue cell, yet Earth exerts a greater influence in the formation cf muscle tissues, bones, and the sense of smell. Water is responsible for the formation of blood, body fluids, and the sense of taste. Fire, is responsible for body temperature, complexion, and the sense of sight. Air is responsible for respiration and the sense of touch. Finally, Space is responsible for body cavities and the sense of hearing.

Figure 2 : The Five Cosmo-Physical Elements Deities of Wood, Fire, Earth, Metal, and Water (Left to Right).

When natural death occurs, these elements, in turn, lose their inherent powers and gradually fade away. Earth is first absorbed by Water and vision becomes blurred. Next, Water is absorbed by Fire and body cavities subsequently dry up. Gradually, Fire is absorbed by Air and there is loss of bodily heat. Finally, Air is absorbed into Space and respiration thus, comes to an end.[11]

Psycho-Physiological Function of the Three *Nyes-pas*[12]

The psycho-physiological function of the Three *Nyes-pas* is further divided into interrelated divisions of fifteen sub-divisions of *rLung* [13], *mKhris-pa*[14], and *Bad-kan* [15] (See Part Two, pp. 52).

Secondly, there are the *Lus-zungs- bDun* or the seven constituents of the body. They are formed through the proper functioning of the fifteen sub-divisions of *rLung, mKhris-pa, Bad-kan*, and the five cosmo-physical elements. The essence of ingested food stuff forms the nutritional essence; the essence of *Dangs-ma* forms blood; the essence of blood forms muscle tissues and so on.

TABLE 2

THE SEVEN BODILY CONSTITUENTS

Essence	Form	Seven Bodily Constituents
Ingested foodstuffs	——	1. *Dangs-ma* (Nutritional essence)
Dangs-ma	——	2. *Khrag* (Blood)
Khrag	——	3. *Sha* (Muscle tissues)
Sha	——	4. *Tshil* (Fatty tissues)
Tshil	——	5. *Rus* (Bone)
Rus	——	6. *rKang* (marrow)
rKang	——	7. *Khu-ba* (regenerative essence)

Finally, as every essence must have its corresponding waste, there are the *Dri-ma gSum* or the three excretory functions of defeacation, urination, and perspiration.

The whole art of healing, therefore involves the proper aligning of the above three divisions, in a dynamic state of equilibrium. If this is accomplished, then the body is said to be in a state of health or free from psycho-physiological disorders. A disequilibrium among three *Nyes-pas*, seven bodily constituents and three excretion constitute a state of ill-health or a diseased state.

AETIOLOGY OF DISEASE AT
THE IMMEDIATE LEVEL

Since a healthy body is in a delicate state of dynamic equilibrium, unwholesome diet, improper lifestyle, seasonal variation, as well as evil spirits influences can easily upset this principle of homeostasis. These four factors are the main causes of disease at the immediate level, and therefore, various measures must persistently be taken in order not to vitiate them.

Diet

The relationship between disease and improper dietary habit is fairly well established. In fact, a majority of health problems, both in the developed and developing countries, can either directly or indirectly be traced to improper dietary habits. Tibetan medicine emphasise the need to take a maximum care of one's diet depending upon one's predisposition, For example, knowing what to eat and in what quantity are the important points to be noted to maintain optimal health.

Obesity, alcoholism, hypertension, arteriosclerosis, diabetes, rheumatism, etc, are problems related in one way or another, with the dietary factors. We also know that, majority of acute and infectious diseases, such as cholera are caused due to unhygenic way of food habits.

Lifestyle

Besides diet, unwholesome lifestyle can also cause the disharmony of the three body principles. Often we neglect the effect of the lifestyle in our day to day health and due to this negligence, we incidently encounter with various kinds of health problems. For example, the cardio-vascular diseases are most commonly found among people who lead sedentary lifestyle and extremely affected by mental stress and strains. Similarly, smoking and drug addiction may cause serious lung diseases and other immunological disorders.

Seasonal

In establishing the relationship between a disorder and seasonal or climatic changes, take the case of the fourth and fifth Tibetan month, which is commonly known as *Sos-ka* (See Table 3). This is a period when the qualities of overall cosmophysical elements are predominantly light and rough. Due to these predominant qualities in the environment, *rlung* accumulates in the body. However, *rlung* aggravates and manifests during summer due to heavy rains and gusty winds besides consumption of light and rough foods such as, consuming too strong tea or indulging in such lifestyles like excessive fasting. Thus, the individual who has not paid proper attention to his/her diet and lifestyle during the late spring, will invariably suffer from a *rlung* disease in summer. In a similar manner, *mKhris-pa* and *Bad-kan* can be accumulated in summer and late winter and then manifest their symptoms in autumn and early spring respectively.

TABLE NO. 3

RELATIONSHIP BETWEEN DISEASE AND THE
SEASONAL CHANGES

Tibetan Month	Seasons	Qualities	Accumulation	Manifes-tation	Pacification
12,1	lower Winter	cool oily heavy	*Bad-kan*	-	-
2,3	Spring	hot	-	*Bad-kan*	-
4,5	Sos-ka	light rough	*rlung*	-	*Bad-kan*
6,7	Summer	oily cool	*mKhris-pa*	*rlung*	-
8,9	Autumn	oily hot	-	*mKhris-pa*	*rlung*
10,11	upper	cool	-	-	*mKhris-pa*

Evil Spirits

Evil spirits can also upset this delicate state of dynamic equilibrium. Their influence is particularly felt in cases where the patient fails to respond to any forms of treatment despite correct diagnosis and treatment.

DIAGNOSIS

The diagnostic techniques in Tibetan medicine are classified into:
(1)   Visual
(2)   Touch
(3)   Interrogation

VISUAL

Visual diagnosis consists of checking the complexion of the skin, the colour and the texture of the blood, nails, sputum, feaces, and other general conditions. Special attention is paid to the condition of the patient's tongue and urine sample. A brief account of the relationship between the state of a tongue and a diseases is given in Table No. 4

TABLE 4

THE TONGUE TEXTURE AND DISEASE OF
THREE *NYES-PAS*

Nyes-pas	Tongue
rlung	Reddish, slightly dry and coarse
mKhris-pa	Thick yellowish coating
Bad-kan	Whitish sticky coating with pale, smooth and moist texture

Urine Examination

It is important to observe certain preliminaries both by the patient and the physician prior to the day of the actual urine examination. For instance, the night before examination, refrain from drinking too much tea, buttermilk or wine to avoid the discolouration of the urine sample. Moreover, the patient should have a good night's rest, refrain from sexual intercourse and mental or emotional stress.

Urine examination.
Note the feature of the container & the stirring stick.

The balanced and healthy urine has a clear light-yellow with a sufficient steam for a longer duration, and medium-sized bubbles appear when stirred vigorously with a stick. Sediments are light and properly diffused. The colour of the urine and the bubbles resume to disappears concentrically from the peripheral to the centre while the steam begins to evaporate. After this transformation, the colour of the urine then changes into white yellow.

Urine examination is carried at three different periods:
(1)   warm
(2)   lukewarm
(3)   cold

For the just voided urine, the physician observes the colour[16], steam, odour, and the bubbles. The sediments and scum are observed when the urine is lukewarm. Finally, when the urine is cooled, the time of transformation, process of transformation and the post transformation changes are noted. The urine characteristic of the three *Nyes-pas* are given in the Table No. 5.

TABLE NO. 5

Nyes-pas	Urine
rlung	Whitish-blue like water with large bubbles when stirred.
mKhris-pa	Yellowish-red with profuse steam, fetid and fast disappearing small bubbles appears when stirred.
Bad-kan	White with distinct odour, saliva like bubbles appears when stirred.

BY TOUCH

Diagnosis by touch refer to the feeling with the physician's hand at various parts or vital points of the patients body. It will help him to identify the degree of body temperature, and to confirm the growth of external cysts or abnormalities.

Sensitivity of certain points in the body gives a good clue

to correlate other major or minor problems related to these points. The most important method employed in Tibetan medicine under this technique is the pulse reading. An in-depth study of the pulse reading is the most essential aspect in order to practice Tibetan medicine.

Pulse reading

It is also important in pulse reading to observe certain pre-liminary dietary and lifestyle restrictions, both by the physician and the patient, one day prior to the day of actual pulse examination. They must, for instance, refrain from physical and mental stress; cut their intake of food and beverages that will affect the nature of pulse. Furthermore, they both must have a good night's rest and try as much as possible, not to disturb the actual state of the disease. After making sure that the required regimens have been observed and that the time is right, the physician then proceeds with his diagnosis. He first, roughly measures the length of the patient's distal pha-lanx of the thumb from the first crease of the wrist and then places his index, middle and ring fingers to feel on the radial artery[17].

The method as well as the specific organs diagnosed by each fingers are illustrated in Fig. 3.

The physician's fingers must be of normal body tempera-ture and should neither be kept too closed nor too far apart. The amount of pressure applied by each finger is as follows:

Finger	Pressure
Index	light
Medius	moderate
Ring	strong

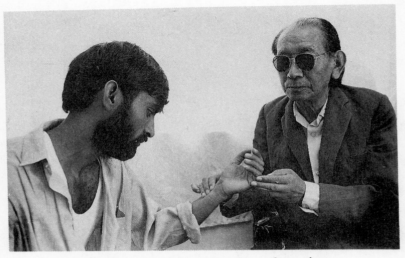

Dr. Lhawang reading the pulse of a patient

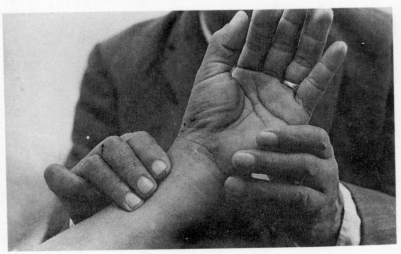

A close up view.
Note the exact position of finger placement during pulse diagnosis.

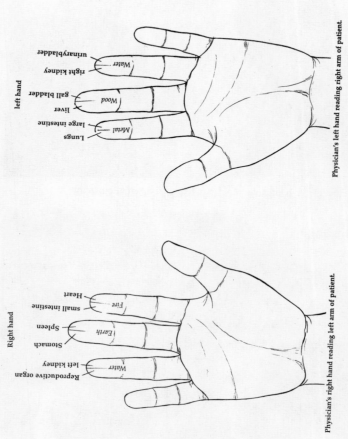

left hand

urinarybladder
right kidney
Water

gall bladder
liver
Wood

large intestine
Lungs
Metal

Physician's left hand reading right arm of patient.

Right hand

Heart
small intestine
Fire

Spleen
Stomach
Earth

Reproductive organ
left kidney
Water

Physician's right hand reading left arm of patient.

Figure 3: Physician's hand exhibiting the finger tip locations used to read the various information about the organs

After going through these preliminaries, the next step is to identify the patient's constitutional pulse. It is simple to know that each and every one has his/her own choice for foods, colours, clothing and other hobbies which decides his/her predispositions or personalities. Similarly, each and every individual is inborn with one of the following three constitutional pulses:

Constitutional Pulse	Characteristics
Male	thick and bulky
Female	thin and taut
Neutral	smooth, flexible in the long continuum.

If the physician, for some reasons, is unable to identify the constitutional pulse, he must ask the patient, since the male pulse can be mistaken for a *rlung*, the female pulse for a *mKhris-pa*, and the neutral pulse for a *Bad-kan* disease.

Once the constitutional pulse has been correctly identified, the physician is then able to classify the diseases into hot and cold categories.

There are six general pulse characteristics of Hot and Cold diseases which are as follows:

Hot	Cold
1. Strong (*Drag*)	1. Weak (*Zhan*)
2. Overflowing (*rGyas*)	2. Sunken (*Bying*)
3. Rolling (*'dril*)	3. Declining (*Gud*)
4. Fast (*mGyogs*)	4. Slow (*Bul*)
5. Taut (*Grims*)	5. Loose (*Lhod*)
6. Firm (*'Khrang*)	6. Empty (*sTong*)

Generally, a hot disease is associated with *mKhris-pa* and a cold disease with *Bad-kan; rlung* is neutral and can either be hot or cold.

The most noticeable pulse qualities of the three *Nye-pas* are as follows:

Nyes-pas	**Pulse Qualities**
rlung	empty, floating with intermittent beats
mKhris-pa	fast, overflowing with taut beats
Bad-kan	sunken, slow with very weak beats

Pulse and the Cosmo-Physical Elements

The influence of cosmo-physical elements on the pulse are revealed primarily through the changing seasonal variations due to the solar-lunar effects on the environment. Before we examine these influences, it is first necessary to understand the relationship among these elements themselves. This is revealed by the 'mother-son' and the 'friend-foe' cycles as illustrated in Fig.4.

Solar and Lunar influence

Within the human body, there are three main subtle channels namely *Roma, rKyang-ma* and *dBu-ma.* The rKyang-ma channel is influenced by the moon (Earth and Water cosmo-physical element), the Roma by the sun (Fire cosmo-physical element) and the dBu-ma by neutral energy (spatial cosmo-physical element). During night time, the lunar influence is stronger and due to this reason, the pulse beat is slower and weaker than the normal. On the other hand, the solar influence is stronger during the day and the pulse beat is faster and stronger. It is for this very reason that the correct time to

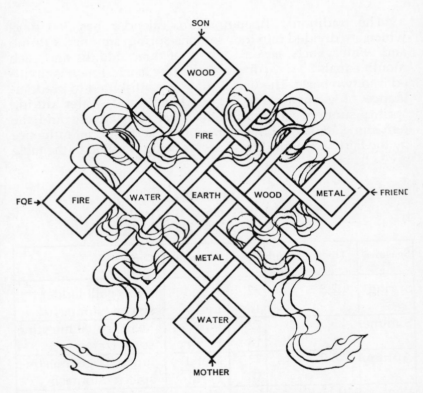

Figure 4 : Mother-Son & Friend-Foe Relationships. The son of Wood is Fire; the son of Fire is Earth etc. The mother of Metal is Earth etc. The Foe of Fire is Water; the Foe of Water is Earth etc. The friend of Metal is Wood; the friend of Wood is Earth etc.

check the pulse is when these two opposite influence are in a dynamic state of equilibrium - this occurs just at the break of dawn, when the lines of one's palm are clearly visible.

Seasonal Influence

The traditional Tibetan Astro. calendar has 360 days which are divided into four seasons-spring, summer, autumn and winter. Each season consists of three months and each month equals 30 days. In pulse reading, each season is divided into two parts. The first 72 days are attributed to predominance of element Wood, Fire, Metal, and Water during spring, summer, autumn, and winter respectively, and the remaining 18 days of the each season exerts special influence by the Earth element. This aspect is being clarified in the table given below.

TABLE NO. 6
SEASONAL INFLUENCE ON THE VITAL
& HOLLOW ORGANS

Seasons	Tibetan Month	Days	Elements	Organs
Spring	1,2,3	72	Wood	liver/gallbladder
		18	Earth	spleen/stomach
Summer	4,5,6	72	Fire	heart/small intestine
		18	Earth	spleen/stomach
Autumn	7,8,9	72	Metal	lungs/large intestine
		18	Earth	spleen/stomach
Winter	10,11,12	72	Water	rt.kidney/urinary bladder lt. kidney/reproductive organs
		18	Earth	spleen/stomach

The first 72 days of spring season exerts a strong influence on the liver/gall bladder pulse when Wood element is predominating the season. This is followed by 18 days when the Earth element exerts special influence on the stomach/spleen pulse.

Similarly, heart/small intestine pulses are predominant during the first 72 days of the summer; lungs/ large intestine pulses are predominant during the first 72 days of the autumn; and kidneys/ urinary bladder/reproductive organ pulses are predominant during the first 72 days of the winter. Earth element predominates during the remaining 18 days of the each season.

It is imperative for the physician to know the exact season while checking the pulse to give a precise diagnosis. For instance, if a physician is not aware that he is checking the pulse during spring, then the stronger liver/gall bladder pulsations may be diagnosed as an ailment. It is precisely for this very reason that the *rGyud-bzhi* elaborately mentions how a physician can identify the seasons through the observation of the stars, birds, trees, etc.

Prognostication

The Tibetan art of pulse reading has a special ways to provide prognosis of the disease as well as other issue related with the family and social well being. An in-depth study of this art reveals the ability of the body to carry within itself a very high level of energy messages that are keenly in tune with the environment. These messages are picked up and passed under the strong cosmic influences. Intimate individual relationships are also used as a parameter through which physician can give various prognosis. We will briefly, examine the use of this knowledge vis-a-vis: (1) the constitutional pulse; (2) mother-son and friend-foe cycles; and (3) the sub-stitutional pulse of the Seven amazing Pulses.[18]

The Constitutional Pulse

As mentioned earlier, the constitutional pulse consists of male, female and the neutral pulse. The following table illus-trates the use of this pulse for prognostication:

TABLE 7
THE CONSTITUTIONAL PULSE

Pulse type	Possessor	Interpretations
Male	Woman	more sons than daughters
Female	Man	long life
Male	Husband & wife	most probably more male offsprings
Female	Husband & wife	most probably more female offsprings
Neutral	Husband & wife	long life; rarely fall sick; superiors will love, whereas inferior person will consistently try to harm them, close relatives may become enemies and their lineage will come to an end.

Mother-Son and Friend-Foe Cycle

Prognostication through the use of the Mother-Son and Friend-Foe cycles are as follows:

Pulse Nature	Prognostication
1. Mother and Seasonal pulses	the best of everything will be showered upon the person.
2. Son pulses	the individual will be very powerful.
3. Friend pulses	the individual will be wealthy.
4. Enemy pulses	the individual will meet enemy or be stricken with a terminal diseases

Now let us study above table in little detail. Suppose an individual is having his pulse prognosticated in spring. This is the season when the strength of Wood element is at its peak and the energies within the liver/gall bladder are at their optimum level. During this season, if the smooth and slow pulse beat of Water (kidneys and genito-urinary organs), which is the mother of the Wood, is predominant under the ring fingers or the seasonal pulse beat, i.e., thin and taut pulse beat of Wood (liver/gall bladder) is predominant, then it signifies that the best of everything will be showered upon that individual. Similar is the application of this method to the summer, autumn, winter, and during the remaining 18 days of each season when Earth element is predominating.

The substitutional pulse

This method involves the assessment of the condition of an individual who is not within easy reach of the physician. This is primarily accomplished by the examination of a close friend or a relative of the patient. For instance, a physician checks a son's pulse in order to determine the health condition of a father who is sick and not within easy reach. Physician could give a good prognosis whether it is possible to help the father or not. The *rGyud-bzhi* explains four ways in using the substitutional pulse:

1. *Checking the son/daughter's pulse when the father/mother is sick*:   If the liver pulse is present, it implies that the father/mother (the patient) can be healed; if absent, it forecasts death. Furthermore, if the mother's pulse (mother of the seasonal pulse) is beating (i.e., if the pulse is being checked during spring, mother's pulse are water-kidney/urinary bladder/reproductive organs pulse), then it is still possible to save the patient. If however, this pulse is weak or missing, then it is an indication of death.

2. *Checking the father/mother's pulse when the son/daughter is sick:*   If the heart pulse is present, it means that the son/daughter (patient) can be healed, if absent ,it forecast death. Moreover, if the son's pulse is beating(i.e. if the pulse is being checked during summer, the son's pulse i.e, Earth-spleen/stomach pulse) then it is possible to save the patient. But if the pulse is missing, it shows that the patient will die.

3. *Checking the wife's pulse when the husband is sick:* Irrespective of seasons, if the liver pulse is present, the patient can be healed, but if it's absent he will die. In terms of elemental calculation, the wife's pulse is the seasonal pulse(i.e,if the pulse is taken during autumn, the Metal element is the wife's pulse). The friend to Metal element i.e, if the Wood which relates to liver and gall bladder pulse, is found strong, the patient will survive, but if it is weak or missing, he will die.

4. *Checking the husband's pulse when the wife is sick:* Irrespective of seasons, if the kidney pulses are present, she can be healed, but if the pulses are absent , she will die. Moreover, in term of elemental calculations, the husband's pulse is the seasonal pulse(i.e, if the pulse is taken during winter , the Water element predominates). The enemy to Water element i.e, if the Earth which relates to spleen and stomach pulse is found strong, she will survive; but if it is weak or missing, she will die.

INTERROGATION

Interrogation, obviously forms the most useful and informative diagnostic technique, enabling the physician to have a clear picture of the patient. Generally, there are three main aspects of interrogation:

1. Finding the causative factors .
2. Finding the site of an illness.
3. Signs and symptoms.

The questions pertaining to the causative factors implies the use of textual words like ; a) what kind of food or drinks one has taken ? b) what kind of physical and mental behaviour being experienced? The wide range of questions assist the physician in getting a clue for the clinical assessment. For example, excessive intake of light and rough food or drinks such as strong tea, pork or indulging in fasting and mental exertions can cause *rlung* disorders. Similarly, excessive intake of hot and sharp food & drinks, such as spices, mutton, alcohol and too much physical activities will lead to the aggravation of *mkhris-pa* disorders. Excessive intake of heavy and oily foods or drinks such as raw fruits, sweets, oily products and staying on wet and damp places are the contributory factors of *Bad-kan* disorders.

Asking about the location of the pains and other abnormalities, is helpful to determine the main site affected by the illness.

Finally, questions relevant to the manifestation of signs and symptoms characterised by the nature of the specific disorders are being asked to correlate with the causes and site of an illness. Therefore, the diagnosis through interrogation serves as the most important clinical aspect of the entire diagnostic techniques.

THERAPEUTICS

Preventive and Curative

The Tibetan art of healing places great emphasis on the gentle method of treatment. Since the cosmo-psycho-physical elements are in a delicate state of dynamic equilibrium, any minor problems caused due to intake of improper diet, unwholesome lifestyle, unfavourable climatic condition, or negative forces of evil spirits, will vitiate the whole homeostatic mechanism. It is for this reason that the first line of health care in Tibetan medicine involves the intake of proper diet and observance of wholesome lifestyles. However, if these two approaches fail to bring about a positive result, then medicines are prescribed. There are various forms of administering medicines which includes decoction, powder, pills, syrup etc. Generally, Tibetan physician starts with a less potent medicine and then gradually increases the potency. The other therapeutic techniques that follows medication includes gentle and drastic eliminative therapies, with surgery being the last resort.

1. Importance of Diet

The importance of dietary regimen is greatly emphasised throughout the *rGyud-bzhi* besides a particular devotion of three full chapters[19] on the topic. These three chapters deals with the classification or variety of foods and beverages and their uses, precautions, and principle of right amount of food intake.

Briefly, food items like grains, meats, oils, and beverages and their specific benefits, depending upon their inherent properties are discussed under special chapters. For instance, grains are classified into those that have ears and legume. Rice, classified among those having ears, is greasy, soothing, cooling and light. It is effective against nausea and diarrhoea.

2. Behavioural approach

The *rGyud-bzhi* classifies the behavioral regimens into routine, seasonal, and incidental. The routine behaviour generally deals with the proper use of one's body, speech, and mind. Occupations or environments which are emotionally disturbing or hazardous are strongly discouraged. Proper adherence to these regular behaviour will not only help in attaining good health and comfortable life, but also to attain longevity and genuine happiness. Emphasis is given to lead a spiritual life in order to minimise ones suffering in this life and ultimately to attain Buddhahood.

With respect to the seasonal behaviour, an individual must be aware of the energy transformation taking place in his body, with respect to the change in environment and must try to harmonize his behaviour with these changes. For instance, during the early winter season (it includes two months), the outside cold environment blocks all the pores of the body and this subsequently, increases the Fire energy. Air further stimulates this heat and consequently, one must consume sufficient food having sweet, sour, and salty tastes or else the bodily constituents will weaken. Early winter is also a period when the nights are longer and one always feels hungry. Little intake of food during this long night season further weakens the seven body constituents (Lus-zungs). To counteract this imbalance, one must massage one's body with sesame oil, take nutritious foods and drinks. Therefore one must carefully observe proper behavioural regimens for the remaining seasons according to the characteristics of the seasonal changes .

The incidental behavioural regimens deal with satiating one's hunger and thirst and the natural urges of yawning, sneezing, urination, defaecation, expulsion of mucus, etc. All these urges must not be suppressed but let nature take its course.

3. Pharmacology

The fundamental tenets of the pharmacology in Tibetan medicine, is intrinsically based on the theory of 'Byung-ba lNga or the five cosmo-physical elements. As mentioned earlier, these energies are not the physico-chemical elements, but concepts dealing more with their inherent subtle qualities rather than their actual state. The subtle qualities of five cosmo-physical elements are given in Table 8.

TABLE NO. 8

THE SUBTLE QUALITIES OF COSMO
PHYSICAL ELEMENTS

Elements	Qualities	Action
Earth	heavy (lci) stable (bstan) blunt (rtul) smooth ('jam) oily (snum) dry (skam)	aggravates Bad-kan pacifies rlung
Water	fluidity (sla) cool (bsil) heavy (lci) blunt (rtul) oily (snum) flexible (mnyen)	aggravates Bad-kan pacifies mKhris-pa
Fire	hot (tsa) sharp (rno) dry (skam) coarse (rtsub) light (yang) oily (snum) mobile (gyo)	aggravates mKhris-pa pacifies Bad-kan
Air	light (yang) mobile (gyo) cold (grang) coarse (rtsub) pale (skya) dry (skam)	aggravates rlung pacifies Bad-kan

These subtle qualities are not only responsible for the material aspects of *rlung, mKhris-pa,* and *Bad-kan,* but also for the six tastes and the three post-digestive tastes, from which the composition, properties, and various actions of a specific medicine are inferred. For their relationships, see Table 9.

TABLE 9

RELATIONSHIP OF 5 COSMO-PHYSICAL ELEMENTS WITH 6 TASTES AND 3 POST DIGESTIVE TASTES[20]

5 C-P Elements	6 Tastes	3 Post-digestive Tastes
Earth+Water	sweet (*mNgar*)	sweet
Earth+Fire	sour (*sKyur*)	sour
Water+Fire	salty (*Lan-tsha*)	sweet
Water+Air	bitter (*Kha-ba*)	bitter
Fire+Air	pungent (*Tsha-ba*)	bitter
Earth+Air	astringent (*bsKa-ba*)	bitter

TABLE 10

EFFECT OF SIX TASTES ON THREE PRINCIPAL ENERGIES

Tastes	Aggravates	Pacifies
sweet	*Bad-kan*	*rlung & mKhris-pa*
sour	*mKhris-pa*	*rlung & Bad-kan*
salty	*mKhris-pa*	*rlung & Bad-kan*
bitter	*rlung & Bad-kan*	*mKhris-pa*
Pungent	*mKhris-pa*	*Bad-kan*
astringent	*rlung & Bad-kan*	*mKhris-pa*

EFFECTS OF THE SIX TASTES ON THE BODY SYSTEM

Sweet Taste

Right intake: Nutritious and agreeable to body, increases seven bodily constituents, promotes physical vigor and vitality, suits to the aged, the juvenile and the emaciated people, soothes the throat; heals ruptured lungs, promotes body weight, heals wound, stimulates the sensory organs, gives clarity to the body complexion and hair, rejuvenates and sustains life, antidote, and pacifies *rlung* and *mKhris-pa* disorder.

Excess: Increases body fat and causes all sorts of *Bad-kan* diseases, decreases body heat, causes obesity, urinary diseases, goitre and induces enlargement of the glands.

Sour Taste

Right intake: Promotes body heat, improves appetite, provides satisfaction, decomposition of food stuffs assists in digestion and absorption of the food materials, when used externally it acts as an antiseptic, opens blocked *rlung* channels.

Excess: Aggravates blood and *mKhris-pa* diseases, causes loose body muscles, blurred vision and vertigo, dropsies, erysipelas, pruritus, boils, thirstiness, and aggravates infections.

Salty Taste

Right intake: Reduces stiffness of the body, cures problems like constipation and opens all vessels within the body, induces perspiration (especially from hot compresses), promotes bodily heat, improves appetite.

Excess: Causes loss of hair, premature white hair and wrinkles, reduces bodily strength, promotes thirst, gives rise to certain skin diseases, aggravates blood and *mKhris-pa* diseases.

Bitter Taste

Right intake: Improves appetite, anti-infective agent, quenches thirst, is an anti-dote, controls certain skin diseases and fainting, stops vomiting, cures infectious diseases and *mKhris-pa*, dries fats, marrow, urine, and feaces, provides determination, cures breast problems and hoarseness of voice.

Excess: Weakens the seven bodily constituents, aggravates *rlung* and *Bad-kan.*

Pungent Taste

Right intake: Used in all throat problems, diptheria, certain skin diseases, dropsy, promotes body heat, assists digestion, improves appetite, opens all body channels, dries up excess fats and drains out excess decomposed matters.

Excess: Reduces semen production, weakens the body, causes contraction of body, shivering, fainting, pain in waist and upper back region.

Astringent Taste

Right intake: It cures blood and *mkhris-p*a diseases, dries excess fats and decomposed matters, heal wounds, promotes lustre to skin complexion.

Excess: Accumulates mucus, causes constipation, distention of the abdomen, cardiac ailments, dries bodily constituents and blocks all body channels.

Volumes have been written on the materia medica of this medical tradition. Apart from the *rGyud-bzhi*, the most well known is the *Dri-med Shel-gong Shel-phreng* written by Geshe Tenzin Phuntsok in 1717 A.D. This text enumerates 2,294 different medicinal substances which according to the *rGyud-bzhi*, are classified into eight different categories. (see Table No.11)

TABLE 11

CLASSIFICATION OF MEDICINAL SUBSTANCES

Classification	Examples	Action+Uses
Rinpoche (Gem)	Turquiose	anti-toxin, cures inflammations in the liver
rDo (stone)	Cinnabar	cures nerve disorders, heals wounds and bone fractures, hepati-tis, lungs infection.
Sa (soils)	Sulphur	anti-prutitic,cures skin diseases, stops bleeding from the nose.
Shing (trees)	Santalum (album. Linn)	antipyretic in general and specially for Pneumonitis, Carditis.
rTsis (mucilaginous)	Cinnamomum camphora	used against acute and chronic fever
Thang (shrubs)	Glycyrrhiza glabra linn	cures pulmonary and vessels (blood and nerve) diseases.
sngo (herbs)	Picrorhiza kurroa Royle	blood coagulant, cures inflammatory diseases of the vital organs.
srog-chags (animal product)	Donkey's tongue	stops diarrhoea

From the above classification of the medicinal substances the following forms of medicine can be prepared:

1. Decoction (*Thang*)
2. Powders (*Phye-ma*)
3. Pills (*Ril-bu*)
4. Medicinal paste (*lDe-gu*)
5. Medicinal butter (*sMan-mar*)
6. Medicinal ash (*Thal-sman*)
7. Concentrated decoction (*Khan-dra*)
8. Medicinal wine (*sMan-chang*)
9. Gem Medicine (*Rin-po-che*)
10. Herbal compounds (*sNgo-sbyor*)

Staff at the Pharmacy Department cleaning
the medicinal ingredients.

Weighing the ingredients according to the formula.

Grinding of ingredients in the pulverizer machine

With coating forms the pills. Here, the Pharmacy staff working on the coating machine.

Drying of pills under the sun

A close up view of the final product

4. External Therapeutic Techniques

Apart from prescribing natural medicine, the physician may also have to depend on other therapeutic techniques. These are again divided into gentle and drastic measures. Massage, hot or cold compresses, mineral-hot- spring therapy and medicinal steam baths are the gentle therapies, and drastic therapies include venesection, cupping, moxibustions, and golden-needle therapy. Surgery is used only as a last resort.

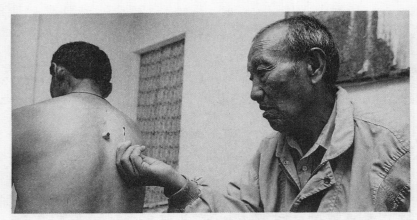

Dr. Tenzin Choedrak, Senior Personal Physician to H.H. the Dalai Lama, using moxibustion at the 6 th vertebra

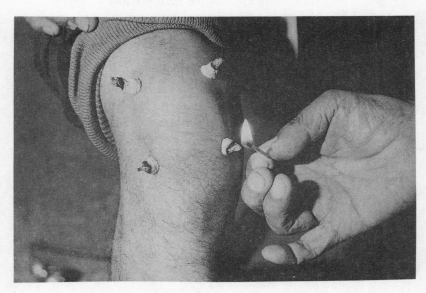

Moxibustion at the knee points of an arthritic patient

CONCLUSION

In recapitulating some of the salient features of Tibetan medical tradition, we note its wholistic approach to medicine. The disorders that afflict man are not just physical, but also cosmo-psychical. The theories of the *Dug-gSum*, *'Byung-ba lNga*, and the three *Nyes-pas* are based on and derives from Buddhist psychology and cosmology. The diagnostic techniques, specially of pulse reading and urology, reveal many salient features of the body which hitherto, have been ignored or underdeveloped. The cardinal lesson on the gentle approach to treatment (with diet, proper mental, emotional, and physical behaviour), as the best medication possible, the use of natural medicine, and the unconditional and compassionate care for the patient are lessons which each and every physician must learn to emulate.

PART TWO

THE ALLEGORICAL TREE

An Allegorical Tree
Depicting the two most important trunks - healthy & diseased body

INTRODUCTION

The second part of the book attempts to confer a comprehensive knowledge of the Tibetan Medical tradition. It illus-
trates the precise meaning of the first part in a little wider
way, by means of using an allegorical tree of the Root Tantra
(*rTsa-rGyud sDong-'grems*), on the basis of the manuscript
written by Rev. Khenrab Norbu (1883-1962). The upper section of the allegorical tree explains the psycho-physiological
aspects of the healthy mind and body entity, dealing mainly
with the proper functions of the three principal energies of
rlung, mKhris-pa and *Bad-kan*. The next section deals with the
aetiology of the diseased body in a sequence manner followed
by the various methods of diagnosis. Finally, the last section
covers the therapeutic measures with special emphasis on the
diet, behaviour, medicine and accessory therapies. It is to be
note, that some repetitions of the first part have been made in
order that the whole explanation of the allegorical tree is not
missed.

ROOT OF AETIOLOGY

The use of illustrations for the Tibetan medical students have been the main method of training from the very beginning of their schooling. This method is helpful in grasping the essential principles of Tibetan medicine to the beginners to adapt with the very common theoretical basis of Tibetan medicine in a short span of time. This is also helpful in reading further extensive texts and commentaries and to put the theoretical knowledge into practical usage.

Root Tantra deals with the synopsis of Tibetan medical theories and practices. It is the heart or the seed of remaining Tantras, because all other theories and practices of Tibetan medicine are based and stem from this text.

From the root of aetiology, there are two trunks. The first trunk deals with the Mind-body in a state of dynamic equilibrium and the second trunk deals with the Mind-Body in dynamic disequilibrium.

Now let us first start the illustration with the help of following Table and then study with their explanations to make it more comprehensible.

ROOT OF AETIOLOGY

Trunk No.	Branches	Leaves	Flowers	Fruits
1	3	25	2	3
2	9	63	-	-
Total	12	88	2	3

TRUNK. NO.1

Mind-Body in Dynamic Equilibrium
(Healthy State)

Branches		Leaves
1.	*Nyes-pa*s	15
2.	Bodily Constituents	7
3.	Three excretions	3
	Total leaves	**25**

As discussed earlier, these twenty five leaves explains the functional aspects of the mind and body. The dynamic equilibrium of these functions ensures optimal health, whereas the disruption of this equilibrium ensures ill health. Let us now study these leaves one by one.

Fifteen aspects of body (*Lus*)
1. Life sustaining *rlung(Srog-'dzin rlung)*
   Seat::   Crown of the head

Pathways: From the pharynx down to the end of the
esophagus

Function: Swallowing of food and drink, respiration,
spitting, sneezing, and eructation, clears
perception of sense organs and helps retention
of memory.

2. Ascending *rlung* (*Gyen-rgyu rlung*)
   Seat: :   Thoracic region
   Pathways: Inside the nose, tongue and throat
   Function: Speech, fair complexion, physical strength,
regulation of body colouring, clarity of
memory, and the spirit of diligence

3. Pervasive *rlung (khyab-byed rlung)*
   Seat :   The heart region
   Pathways: Circulates throughout the body
   Function: Proper functioning of muscle tissues, lifting,
walking, stretching, contraction, opening and
closing of orifices.

4. Fire like *rlung (Me-mnyam rlung)*
   Seat :   The stomach
   Pathways: throughout the alimentary canal
   Function: Assists in digestion, absorption and metabolic
activities of bodily constituents

5. Downward Cleansing *rlung (Thur-sel rlung)*
   Seat::   Perineal region
   Pathway: Through the large intestine, urinary bladder,
sex organs, and the thighs
   Function: Helps defaecation, urination, ejaculation of
sperm and menstrual blood, and opening and
contractile activity of the uterus

6. Digestive *mkhrispa(mKhris-pa 'Ju-byed)*
   Seat::   Resides at the stomachal region.

Function: Responsible for digestion, the separation of certain essential nutrients from ingested food stuffs, promotes bodily heat, facilitates the proper functioning of the remaining four types of *mKhris-pa*

7. Determining *mKhrispa (mKhris-pa sGrub-byed)*
    Seat::   Resides in the heart region
    Function: Responsible for accomplishing the mind's initial thoughts of desire, ambition, pride etc.

8. Complexion clearing *mKhris-pa (mKhrispa mDangs-sgyur)*
    Seat::   Resides in the liver
    Function: Responsible for the red colouring of blood and muscle tissues etc.

9. Sight *mKhrispa (mKhris-pa mThong-byed)*
    Seat::   Resides in the eyes
    Function: Responsible for vision

10. Colour regulating *mKhris-pa (mKhris-pa mDog-gsal)*
    Seat::   Resides in the skin
    Function: Responsible for skin colour

11. Supporting *Badkan (Bad-kan rTen-byed)*
    Seat::   Resides around the thoracic region
    Function: Regulates bodily fluids, supports the other four types of *Bad-kan*

12. Decomposing *Badkan (Bad-kan Myag-byed)*
    Seat::   Resides in the epigastric region
    Function: Responsible for breaking down of solid foodstuffs into semi-liquid state

13. Experiencing *Bad-kan (Bad-Kan Myong-byed)*
    Seat::   Resides in the tongue
    Function: Responsible for experiencing the tastes

14. Satisfying *Badkan (Bad-kan Tsim-byed)*
    Seat::   Resides in the head

Function: Responsible for the satisfaction of sense
                organs
15. Connecting *Badkan (Bad-kan 'Byor-byed)*
    Seat::   Resides in all bodily joints
    Function: Responsible for connecting various body
                joints, flexion and contraction of body limbs

Seven Bodily Constituents (*Lus-zungs-bdhun*)

1. *Dangs-ma* :   essential nutrients from ingested foodstuffs
2. *Khrag* :   blood is formed through the essence of
              Dangsma
3. *Sha* : muscle is formed through the essence of blood
4. *Tshil* : fat is formed through the essence of muscle tissues
5. *Rus* :   bone is formed through the essence of bodily fats
6. *rKang* :   marrow is formed through the essence of bones
7. *Khu-ba* :   regenerative fluids are formed through the
              essence of marrow

Three Excretions (*Dri-ma gSum*)

1. Defaecation (*bShang*)
2. Urination (*gCin*)
3. Perspiration (*rNgul*)

Two Flowers
1. Health
2. Long life

Three Fruits
1. High spiritual life
2. Wealth
3. Happiness

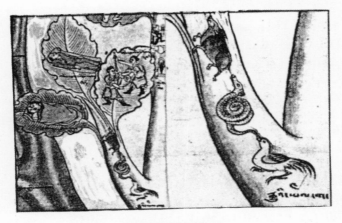

TRUNK NO. 2

Mind-Body in dynamic disequilibrium
(Diseased Dtate)

Primordial causes of three *Nyes-pas*
1. *'Dhod-chags* causes *rlung*
2. *Zhe-sdang* causes *mKhris-pa*
3. *gTi-mug* causes *Bad-kan*

Immediate causes of Three Disorders
1. Imbalance Diet
2. Improper Bahaviour
3. Seasonal changes.
4. Evil spirits.

General Pathways of Diseases[1]
1. Skin - Initially, the disease spreads on the skin
2. Muscle tissues -Next, it develops in the muscle tissues
3. Vessels - Then it moves through the vessel (Blood
   vessels and nerves)

4. Bones - Then it affects the bones
5. *Don-lNga* (5 vital organs) -Finally descends to : (1) heart; (2) liver; (3) lungs; (4) spleen; and (5) kidneys.
6. *sNod-drug* (6 hollow organs) -Disorder then falls into the six hollow organs of: (1) stomach: (2) large intestine; (3) gall bladder; (4) urinary bladder;   (5) small intestine; (6) and reproductive organs.

General Location of Three *Nyes-pas*
1. *Bad-kan* is located in the upper part of the body
2. *mKhris-pa* is located in the middle part of the body
3. *rlung* is generally seated in the waist and hip region

Specific Pathways of Three *Nyes-pas*
rlung moves through:
1. Bones
2. Ears
3. Skin
4. Heart- blood vessels & nerves
5. Large intestine

mKhris-pa moves through:
1. Blood
2. Eyes
3. Sweat
4. Liver
5. Gall bladder and small intestine

Bad-kan moves through:
1. *Dangs-ma*, muscle tissues, fat, marrow, regenerative fluids
2. Nose and tongue
3. Passages connected with urination and defaecation

4. Lungs, spleen, kidneys
5. Stomach and urinary bladder

General Conditions favourable for three *Nyes-pas*

Age
1. Aged person has the natural condition of the *rlung*, wherein the overall energies of the body are very much diminished and hence are susceptible to *rlung* disorders.

2. Adults have a natural condition of *mKhris-pa*, wherein the overall energies of the body are at their peak and hence are susceptible to the *mkhris-pa* disorders

3. Children has the natural condition of *Bad-kan* wherein the overall energies of the body are just developing and hence are susceptible to *bad-kan* disorders.

Place
4. *rlung* develops and accumulates in cold and windy regions
5. *mKhris-pa* develops and accumulates in hot and dry regions
6. *Bad-kan* develops and accumulates in wet and humid regions.

Time
7. *rlung* disorder manifests during summer, evening and break of the dawn
8. *mKhris-pa* disorder manifests during autumn, noon and mid night
9. *Bad-kan* disorder manifests during spring, dusk and morning

Nine disorders of Fatal effects
1. Exhaustion of one's Life's span, karma, and
    merits
2. The simultaneous combination of both the hot
    and cold disorders resulting in a terminal state, on
    account of the counteraction of treatment
3. The disease ultimately becomes acute, due to treat-
    ment being identical to the nature of disease.
4. Any form of weapons or missiles affecting the vul-
    nerable or vital organs or parts of the body
5. *rlung* is beyond treatment which affects the life force-
    rlung dBu-ma, thus respiration comes to an end
6. A hot disease which has gone beyond its limit of
    treatment
7. A cold disease which has fallen below its recovery
    limit
8. Body becoming too weak for treatment
9. Evil spirits subduing life force and vital energy of
    the body system

12 adverse effects
1. *rlung* treatment in excess which pacify the *rlung* but
    mKhris-pa rises
2. *rlung* treatment in excess which pacify the *rlung* but
    Badkan rises
3. Due to wrong treatment, *rlung* is not controlled
    besides rise in *mkhris-pa*
4. Due to wrong treatment, *rlung* is not controlled
    besides rise in *Bad-kan*
5. *mKhris-pa* treatment in excess which pacify *mkhris-pa*
    but *rlung* rises
6. *mkhris-pa* treatment in excess which pacify *mkhris-pa*

but *Bad-kan* rises

7. Due to wrong treatment, *mKhris-pa* is not controlled besides rise in *rlung*

8. Due to wrong treatment, *mkhris-pa* is not controlled besides rise in *Bad-kan*

9. *Bad-kan* treatment in excess which pacify *Badkan* but *rlung* rises.

10. *Badkan* treatment in excess which pacify *Badkan* but *mKhris-pa* rises

11. Due to wrong treatment, *Bad-ka*n is not controlled besides rise in *rlung*

12. Due to wrong treatment, *Badkan* is not controlled besides rise in *mKhris-pa*

Summary

1. Cold: *rlung* and *Bad-kan*, like water are cool by nature

2. Hot: blood and *mKhris-pa*, like fire are hot by nature

(micro-organism and serous fluids are neutral by nature and can be either hot or cold depending on the predominance of the *Nyes-pas*).

ROOT OF DIAGNOSIS

1. Visual Diagnosis

(a) Tongue

(i)	*rlung* tongue -	Reddish, its texture is slightly dry and rough
(ii)	*mKhris-pa* tongue -	Covered with a thick light yellow coating.
(iii)	*Bad-kan* tongue -	Whitish with sticky coating , lustreless, smooth, and moist texture

(b) Urine

(i)	*rlung* urine -	Like water and big bubbles appear when stirred
(ii)	*mKhris-pa* urine-	Reddish yellow with lot of vapour, malodorous and fast disappearing bubbles appear when stirred
(iii)	*Bad-kan* urine -	Whitish, less odour and steam, saliva-like bubbles appear when stirred

2. Pulsology

(i)	*rlung* Pulse :	Floating, empty when pressed and halts irregularly
(ii)	*mKhris-pa* Pulse :	Fast, overflowing and taut.
(iii)	*Bad-kan* Pulse :	Sunken, weak and slow

3. Interrogation
rlung
Causes
(i)   Excessive intake of light and rough foods, and indulging in such behaviour.

Signs & Symptoms
(ii)   Yawning and shivering
(iii)   Frequent sighing and stretching of limbs
(iv)   Cold chills
(v)   Pain, specially in the hips, waist, bones, and joints
(vi)   Uncertain shifting pain
(vii)   Empty emesis
(viii) Dullness of the senses
ix)   Unrest mental state
(x)   Pain when hungry

Response
(xi)   Responding well to the oily and nutritious diet and life style

mKhris-pa
Causes
(i)   Excessive intake of sharp and heat producing foods, and indulging in such behaviour

Signs & Symptoms
(ii)   Bitter taste in mouth
(iii)   Headache
(iv)   Surface temperature or body heat
(v)   Pain in upper region of the body
(vi)   Pain after the food has been digested

Response
(vii)   Responding well to the cooling diet and life
           style.

Bad-kan
Causes
(i)   Excessive intake of heavy and greasy foods, and
           indulging in such behaviour

Signs & Symptoms
(ii)   Loss of appetite
(iii)   Indigestion
(iv)   Frequent emesis
(v)   No taste in food
(vi)   Stomach feels full even though there is no food
(vii)   Frequent eructation
(viii)   Discomfort after eating
(ix)   Lethargy
(x)   Feeling of cold inside as well as outside the
           body

Response
(xi)   Responding well to the warm food and
           lifestyle

ROOT OF THERAPEUTICS

I. DIET
rlung Food
(i)   Mustard oil
(ii)   Aged butter
(iii)   Molasses
(iv)   Allium sativum Linn. (garlic)
(v)   Allium sepa Linn. (onion)
(vi)   Aged meat

Beverage for *rlung*
(i)   Warm milk
(ii)   *Zan-chang*[2] made from Angelica sp. and
         Polygonatum cirrhifolium Royle
(iii)   Wine from molasses
(iv)   Wine from crushed bone

mKhris-pa Food

(i)   Curd from cow or goat's milk[3]

(ii)   Buttermilk from cow or goat's milk[4]

(iii)   Fresh butter

(iv)   Goat meat

(v)   Porridge made from fresh barley

(vi)   Stew made from dandelion leaves (Taraxacum sp.)

(vii)   Stew made from Taraxacum officinale Web.

mKhris-pa - Beverage

(i)   Boiled plain water

(ii)   Cool water from snow and glacier

(iii)   Boiled cold water

Bad-kan - Food

(i)   Mutton

(ii)   Yak meat

(iii)   Fish

(iv)   Honey

(iv)   Gruel made from aged barley that is grown in dry areas

Bad-kan - Beverage

(i)   Curd and buttermilk from Dri's milk (female Yak)

(ii)   Concentrated chang (a Tibetan beverage)

(iii)   Boiled hot water

II. BEHAVIOUR

Behaviour for *rlung*
(i)   Living in dimmed apartment and warm region
(ii)   Enjoying the company of once close and dear
         friend

Behaviour for *mKhris-pa*
(i)   Living in cool areas or by the seaside
(ii)   Relaxing without disturbance

Behaviour for *Bad-kan*
(i)   Regular exercise
(ii)   Living in warm and well-heated rooms

III. MEDICINE

Medicines for *rlung*
Tastes
(i)   Sweet (molasses)
(ii)   Sour (matured *chang*)
(iii)   Salty (sodium chloride)

Inherent qualities :-
(i)   Oily (Aquilaria agollocha Roxb.)
(ii)   Heavy (black salt)
(iii)   Smooth (Rubus idaeopsis Focke.)

Medicine for *mKhrispa*
Tastes
(i)   Sweet (Vitis vinifera Wall.)
(ii)   Bitter (Herpetospermum pedunculosum)
(iii)   Astringent (Santalum album Linn.)

Inherent qualities
(i)   Cool (Cinnamomum camphora Nees et. Eberm.)
(ii)   Liquid (Cassia fistula Linn.)
(iii)   Blunt (Bambusa textilis)

Medicine for *Badkan*
Tastes
(i)   Pungent (Piper nigrum Linn.)
(ii)   Sour (Punica granatum Linn.)
(iii)   Astringent (Terminalia Bellerica)
Inherent qualities
(i)   Sharp (rock salt)
(ii)   Coarse (Hippophae rhamnoides Linn.)
(iii)   Light(Capsicum Fructescens.)

Soup that pacifies *rlung*
(i)   Bone soup
(ii)   Soup extracted from meat, butter, molasses, and aged
         chang
(iii)   Broth from aged sheep's head

Medicinal butters that pacifies *rlung*
(i)   Medicinal butter with Myristica fragrans, Houtt. (nut-
meg)   as its main ingredient.
(ii)   Medicinal butter with Allium sativum Linn. (garlic) as
         its main ingredient.
(iii)   Medicinal butter with the three fruits (Termi
         nalia chebula Retz., Terminalia belerica Roxb.,
         and Emblica officinalis Gaertn) as its main
         ingredients.
(iv)   Medicinal butter with the five roots (Withania
         somniferra, Tribulus terrestris Linn., Angelica sp.,

Polygonatum cirrhifolium (Wall.) Royle, Asparagus racemocus) as its main ingredients.

(v)   Medicinal butter with Aconitum balfouri Wall as its main ingredient.

Decoctions that pacifies *mKhris-pa*

(i)   Decoctions with Inula racemosa Hook, as its main ingredient.

(ii)   Decoctions with Tinospora cordifolia Miers as its main ingredient.

(iii) Decoctions with Swertia Chirata as its main ingredient.

(iv)   Decoctions with the three fruits (Terminalia chebula Retz., Terminalia belerica Roxb., and Emblica officinalis Gaertn) as its main ingredients.

Medicinal powders that pacifies *mKhris-pa*

(i)   Medicinal powders with Cinnamomum camphora as its main ingredient.

(ii)   Medicinal powders with Santalum album Linn as its main ingredient.

(iii) Medicinal powders with Carthamus tinctorius Linn as its main ingredient.

(iv)   Medicinal powders with Bambusa textilis as its main ingredient.

Medicinal pills that pacifies *Bad-kan*

(i)   Medicinal pills with Aconitum heterophyllum Wall as its main ingredient.

(ii)   Medicinal pills with various salts such as sodium chloride, black salt, rock salt as its main ingredients.

Medicinal powders that pacifies *Bad-kan*

(i)   Medicinal powders with Punica granatum Linn as its main ingredient.

(ii)   Medicinal powders with Rhododendron aff. cephalantum as its main ingredient.

(iii)   Medicinal powders whose compound is known as *rGod-ma Kha* (strongest heat-producing medicine).

(iv)   Medicinal powders with calcinated salts as its main ingredients.

(v)   Medicinal powders with calcinated calcite as its main ingredient.

Suppositories for *rlung*

(i)   *sLe-'jam*: A mild enema which involves the procedure of inserting medicine through rectum to eliminate the *rlung* disorder.

(ii)   *bKru-'jam*: moderate enema consisting of *sLe-'jam* but with the addition of another formula which is given to the patient who lies on his back while the physician gently taps the soles of the patient to eliminate the *mKhrispa-rlung* combined disorders.

(iii)   *bKru-ma-slen*: strong enema , another additional formula added to *bKru-'jam* which is then given to the patient and the physician holds the patient by the feet and shakes up and down to eliminate the *badkan-rlung* combined disorders.

Purgatives for *mKhris-pa*

(i)   *sPyi-bshal*: a gentle purgative as part of the initial preparation

(ii)   *sGos-bshal*: specific purgative is given after which, the patient must rinse his mouth

(iii)   *Drag-shal:* a strong purgative, if induces vomiting
         which must be suppressed by either pressing the
         patient by the shoulders or pulling his hair
(iv)   *'Jam-bshal*: finally, a hot compress is put on the
         patient's stomach

Emetics for *Bad-kan*
(i)   *Drag-skyugs:* the patient bends his knees up to
         the stomach in a squatting posture.
(ii)   *'Jam-skyugs*: the patient covers himself with warm
         clothes and then sits in a squatting posture.

IV ACCESSORY THERAPEUTIC TECHNIQUES
rlung
(i)   Massage with butter or Sesamum indicum Linn.
(ii)   *Horgi-Metsa*: put Carum carvi Linn. in cloth and
         immerse in hot oil and compress it at various *rlung*
         points.

mKhris-pa
(i)   Keep the patient under thick coverings, so that
         the body perspires.
(ii)   Venesection at various points of the body.
iii)   Placing the patient under a waterfall or a cold
         shower.

Bad-kan
(i)   Giving a hot compress on the stomach, by heated salt
         wrapped in cloth.
(ii)   Moxibustions at specific points on the bodily joints.

NOTES

First Part

1.   It is tradition to begin with a Sanskrit title to any major Tibetan Texts in order to make it more authentic and valuable. It's also believed to be auspicious to use Sanskrit, since Buddha himself taught in that language and even to these day it is used for various book titles.

2.   *"gSang-ba-Man-ngag-gi-rGyud"* implies that this medical tradition is an esoteric tantric teaching whose genuine knowledge and practice leads one directly to the state of ultimate bliss or nirvana. In fact, this medical teaching is one of the highest Yoga tantras(*rNal-'byor-bla-med-kyi-rgyud*). Practitioner must be well prepared and formally initiated by the masters, else he may face various obstacles in life. Highly spiritual life and generating genuine compassion and love for the patient are necessary in order to practice this tantric medical teaching.

3.   Rechung Rinpoche, Tibetan Medicine, Wellcome Institute, London, 1973.

4.   Both the elder and the younger Yuthogs are considered to be reincarnations of the Medicine Buddha. For a full account of the life story of the Elder Yuthog Yonten Gonpo, see *Darmo-sMan-ram-pa blo-bZang Chos-grag's* edition of *gYuthog Yonten mGon-po rNying-ma'i rNam thar bKa'-rGya-ma gZhi-brjid rin- po-che'i gter-mdzod*. He was the founder of our first parent institute, the Tanadug Medical College in Kongpo Menlung in Tibet.

5.   *"rGyud-bzhi"* or the four Tantras are :
  i)   *rtsa rGyud*-Root Tantra.
  (ii)   *bshad rGyud*-Explanatory Tantra.
  (iii)   *Man-nGag-rGyud*-Quintessential tantra.
  (iv)   *Phyi-ma-rGyud* - The Last Tantra. *rGyud-bzhi* is
  the most authoritative fundamental treatise on
  traditional Tibetan medicine.

6.   *Cha-lag-bcho-brgyad*, Lhasa Zhol Press. 1893.

7.   According to Zurkar Lodoe Gyalpo, *Rig-pa'i Ye-shes* is
the Younger Yuthog, while *Yid-las-sKye* is his favourite disciple, Sumthon Yeshi.

8.   Corresponds to Tridoshas in the Indian Ayurvedic
medicine.

9.   According to the Buddhist doctrine of the wheel of
life, all non-enlightened beings in the six realms of existence
(i.e., the realms of dieties, titans, humans, animals, hungry
spirits and hell) are afflicted with the imperfections of the
three fundamental poisons (*Dug-gSum*).   These afflictions,
like shadow are ever present within every being and can only
be eliminated   through   the   genuine   practice   of   the
Dharma.

10 .   Grasping at the self; the conceptual misapprehension
of a truly existence self; as a person or a natural phenomenon.

11.   Explanatory Tantra, chapter - 7 *rGyud-bzhi*, Dharamsala, TMC, 1971.

12 .   *rlung, mKhrispa* and *badkan*, the three principal energies of the body are called the three *Nyes-pas*. It is to be note
that these principal energies are directly linked with the
Cosmo-physical elements of Air, Fire and Water respectively.
The dynamic equilibrium of the three *Nyes-pas* is healthy
mind and body entity. If this balance is disturbed it is said to
be unhealthy or a diseased body.

13.   *rlung* is one of the three principal energy of the body
which manifest the nature of Air element. It is characterised
by rough, light, cold, subtle, hard and mobile. The five sub-
division or aspects of *rlung* are:
    i) Life sustaining *rlung*.
    (ii) Ascending *rlung*
    (iii) Pervasive *rlung*
    (iv) Fire like *rlung*
    (v) Downward voiding *rlung*
    Although, they have their specific functions, but gen-
erally, they are all responsible for the physical and mental
activities, respiration; expulsion of urine, faeces, fetus, men-
struation, spitting, burping, speech, gives clarity to sense
organs, sustain life by means of acting as a medium between
mind and body. These five *rlung* resides at the five main energy centres of crown, throat, heart, navel and genital chakras
respectively.

14   Like *rlung*, it is one of the three principal energy of the
body which basically has the nature of fire. *mKhrispa* is characterised by oily, sharp, hot, light, fetid, purgative and fluidi-
ty. Generally, it is responsible for hunger, thirst, digestion and
assimilation, promotes bodily heat, gives lustre to body complexion and provide courage and determination. Its five sub
divisions or aspects are:

(i)   Digestive *mkhris-pa*
(ii)   Colour regulating *mkhris-pa*
(iii)   Accomplishing *mkhris-pa*
(iv)   Sight *mKhris-pa*
(v)   Complexion clearing *mKhris-pa*

15.   *Bad-kan* is one of the three principal energy of the body which is cold in nature and is characterised by oily, cool, heavy, blunt, smooth, firm and sticky. Generally, *badkan* is responsible for firmness of the body, stability of mind, induces sleep, connects bodily joints, generate tolerance and lubricates the body. The five sub-divisions of *bad-kan* are:

(i)   Supporting *bad-kan*
(ii)   Decomposing *bad-kan*
(iii)   Expressing *bad-kan*
(iv)   Satisfying *bad-kan*
(v)   Connective *bad-kan*

16.   It is important to use white container for observing colour of the urine.

17.   The site at the arteria radialis is likened to a central market place, blood and *rlung* (compare to a trader) constantly circulate throughout the body and return back with information about the conditions of various organs & other parts of the body. It is also the most appropriate place, being not too far away nor too close to the heart.

18 .   The other amazing pulses that deals with the prognostication are:

(i)   Family welfare.
(ii)   Arrival of the guest..
(iii)   Harms from the enemies.

(iv)   Wealth.

(v)   Harms from the evil spirits.

(vi)   Sex of an unborn child.

19 .   Second tantra, Chapter 16-18, *rGyud-bzhi*, Dharamsala,
TMC, 1971

20 .   Compare this with the following Ayurvedic combina-
tions:

    1)   Earth + Water = Sweet
    2)   Earth + Fire = Sour
    3)   Earth + Air = Astringent
    4)   Water + Fire = Salt
    5)   Fire + Air = Acrid
    6)   Air + Space = Bitter

Second Part

1.   It refers to the general entrance of the diseases in rela-
tion to their corresponding path ways. It does not imply that
every disease follow the same sequence as described, since
there are diseases of contrary sequence as well.

2.   A type of beverage prepared with cooked grains.

3,4   Medical text listed them under food.

REFERENCES

1. *Bod-ljongs rGyun-spyod Krung-dbyi'i sMan-rigs,* Peking,1973.

2. Das, B and L Kashyap - Basic Principles of Ayurveda New Delhi: Concept Publishing Co., 1980.

3. Dorland's Pocket Medical Dictionary; 22 nd ed, Philadelphia, W.B. Saunders, 1977.

4. GYATSO, Desi Sangye - *rGyud - bzhi'i gsal - byed Vaidurya sNgon-po.* Lhasa; Zhol Press 1893.

5. Norbu, Khenrab - *rtsa-rGyud sDong-'grms gSo-rig rGya-mtso'i sNying-po,* Sarnath, Tibetan Monastery Press, 1966.

6. Sharma, P.V. - Introduction to Dravyaguna Varanasi, Chaukhambha Orientalia, 1976.

7. YUTHOG Yonten Gonpo (Elder) - *bDud-rtsi-sNying-po Yan-lag brGyad-pa gSang-ba Man-nNag gi rGyud.* Lhasa, Chakpori Press, 1888.

8. ZURKAR Lodroe Gyalpo - *rtsa bshad 'grel-pa Mes-po'i Zhal-lung* Lhasa , Zhol Press, 1893.

9. Wangdue - *gSo-ba-rig-pa'i-tsig-mdzod-gYu-thog-dGong-rGyan. Me-rigs-dpe-sKrun-khang,* 1982.

10. C. Karma - *bDud-rtsi-sMan gyi 'Khrungs dpe legs bshad Nor-bu'i phreng-mdzes,* Tibet, 1993.

11. DEUMAR, Tenzin Phuntsok - *sMan-gyi Nus-pa Dri-med Shel - Phreng,* Dharamsala, 1994.

12. Gongmen Kunchog *Deleg - gSo-rig dGos pa Kun -*

byung, Leh - Tashigang, 1971.

13. Sogpo Lungrik Tender - *rGyud -bzi brda-don bkrol-ba-rNam-rgyal A ru-ra yi phreng-ba.*

14. Gyatso, Desi Sangye - *Vaidurya dkar-po* New Delhi. Tsepal Taikhang, 1972.

15. Das, Chandra - Tibetan English Dictionary New Delhi; Book Faith India, 1992.

16. Rigzin, Tsepak - Tibetan English Dictionary of Buddhist Terminology. Dharamsala, LTWA ,1986.

17. N. Victoria - Webster's New World Dictionary, New York, Simon and Schuster, Inc., 1991.

18. Roper, Nancy - Pocket Medical Dictionary 13th Edition. Edinburg, 1978.

TRANSLITERATION

We have used Wylie transliteration system in this edition, since it is the most simplest method for translitering Tibetan. The following chart illustrates the Wylie transliteration system for the base letters and four vowels.

ཀ་ ka	ཁ་ kha	ག་ ga	ང་ nga
ཙ་ ca	ཆ་ cha	ཇ་ ja	ཉ་ nya
ཏ་ ta	ཐ་ tha	ད་ da	ན་ na
པ་ pa	ཕ་ pha	བ་ ba	མ་ ma
ཙ་ tsa	ཚ་ tsha	ཛ་ dza	ཝ་ wa
ཞ་ zha	ཟ་ za	འ་ 'a	ཡ་ ya
ར་ ra	ལ་ la	ཤ་ sha	ས་ sa
	ཧ་ ha	ཨ་ a	
ཨི་ i	ཨུ་ u	ཨེ་ e	ཨོ་ o

CONTENTS OF RGYUD-BZHI

1. *rtsa-rGyud*
(Root Tantra - 6 chapters)

1. *Gleng-gzhi:* The original (Mandala) basis of discourse on medicine, a brief description on the five excellences of dharma, perod, teacher, abode and retinue.

2. *Gleng-slong:* Enumeration of the subject of discourse, i.e., the chapters of the *rGyud-bzhi*.

3. *gZhi:* The basis of mind-body in dynamic equilibrium and disequilibrium representing healthy and diseased body.

4. *Ngos-'dzin:* Diagnosis and symptoms of the disorders.

5. *gSo-thabs:* Therapeutic methods - dealing with diet, behaviour, medication and accesory therapies.

6. *rtsis-kyi-le'u:* Synopsis of the Root Tantra.

II *bshad-rGyud*
(Explanatory Tantra - 32 Chapters)

1. *bshad-pa'i-sdom:* Summary of the Explanatory Tantra.

2. *Chags-tsul:* Embryology.

3. *'Dra-dpe:* Basic anatomy in similes

4. *gNas-lugs* : Quantitative anatomy dealing with the proportion of bodily constituents, channels (nerves and blood vessels) and the important passages within the body.

5. *lus-kyi mtsan-nYid*: Basic physiology of mind-body.

6. *dbye-ba* : Classification of the body in terms of sex, age, temperament and disease.

7. *'jig - ltas* : Signs of death.

8. *nad-kyi-rGyu* : Primordial causes of disorders.

9. *nad-kyi-rKyen* : Immediate causes of disorders.

10. *nad Zhugs-tsul*: Manners of how diseases enter human body.

11. *Nad-kyi mtsan-nyid*: The characteristic of rlung, mkhrispa and badkan disorders.

12.. *Nad-kyi-dye-ba:* Classification of disease

13. *rGyun-Spyod:* The routine behaviour.

14. *Dus-spyod* : Seasonal behaviour

15. *gNas-sKabs Spyod-lam*: Incidental behaviour.

16. *Zas-tsul* :   Dietetics, deals with the knowledge of qualities and use of particular foods and drinks.

17. *Zas-bsdam* :   Dietary restriction on incompatible combination of food & drinks.

18. *Zas-tshod ran - pa*:   Dietary regimen dealing with right intake of food & drinks.

19. *sMan-gyi-ro* :   Taste of medicinal substances.

20. *sMan-gyi-Nus-pa* : Inherent qualities of medicinal substances.

21. sMan-gyi-sbyar-thabs: Pharmacology.

22. *Cha-byad*: Different therapeutic instruments.

23. *Mi-na-gNas:* Prophylactic regimens of diet, behaviour and medication.

24. *Nyes-pa-dNgos-ston* : General techniques for correct diagnosis

25. *Ngan-gYo-Skyon-brtag:* Techniques for gaining patients confidence.

26. *sPang-blang Mu-bzhi:* Four diagnostic techniques to verify whether the patient can be healed or not.

27. *gSo-tsul-sPyi* : General healing techniques.

28. *Khyad-par gSo-thabs:* Specific healing techniques.

29. *gSo-thabs-gNyis* : Two healing techniques: methods for gaining & losing weight.

30. *gSo-thabs-dNgos* :The actual treatment of rlung, mkhris-pa and bad-kan disorder.

31. *sMan-pa'i-le'u* : The required qualities and commitments of a physician.

III - *Man-ngag-rgyud*
(Quintessential Tantra 92 Chapters)

1. *Zhus-pa* :Requesting to reveal the quintessential tantra.

2. *rlung* : Diagnosis and treatment of rlung disorder.

3. *mkhris-pa* : Diagnosis and treatment of mkhris-pa disorder.

4. *bad-kan* : Diagnosis and treatment of bad-kan disorder.

5. *'dus-nad* : Diagnosis and treatment of bad-kan smugpo disorder - a complicate gastro intestinal disease.

6. *ma-zhu-ba* : Indigestion

7.   *skran* : Tumour

8.   *Skya-rbab:* Dropsy, at the initial stage.

9.   *'Or* : Dropsy of the skin Vesicles.

10.   *dmu-chu* : Dropsy of the internal organs.

11.   *gChong-chen Zad-byed*: Chronic metabolic disorder resulting in a wasting of bodily constituents.

12.. *tsha-ba-spyi* :   General fever.

13.   *gal-mdo* : The important approach in distinguishing a hot and cold disorder.

14.   *ri-thang-mtsams*: The junction between mountain and plain. This refers to an art of differentiating a junction between hot and cold disorder.

15.   *ma-sMin-tshaba* :Unripened fever

16.   *rGyas-tshad* :   Extreme fever.

17.   *stong-tshad*:   Empty fever.

18.   *gab-tshad* :   Hidden fever.

19.   *rNying-tshad* : Chronic fever.

20.   *rNogs-tshad*:   Complicate fever.

21.   *'Grams tshad* :   Spreaded fever

22.   *'Khrugs-tshad*:   Disturbed fever

23.   *rims-tshad* :   Epidemic fever

24.   *brum-pa* :   Small pox.

25.   *rGyu-gZer* :   Intestinal infection, such as colitis.

26.   *gag-lhog* :   Inflammation associated with throat and mucle tissues.

27.   *Cham-pa* :   Catarrh.

28.   *mGo-nad* :   Diseases of the head.

29.   *mig-nad* :   Ophthalmic disease

30.   *rNa-nad* :   Diseases of the ear.

31.   *sNa-nad* :   Nasal disease.

32.   *Kha-nad* :   Disease of the mouth.

33.   *lba-ba* :   Goitre

34.   *sNying-nad* :   Cardiac disease

35.   *gLo-nad* :   Pulmonary disease.

36.   *mchin-nad* :   Hepatic disease.

37. *mcher-nad* :   Splenic disease.

38. *mKhal-nad* :   Renal disease.

39. *pho-ba'i-nad* :   Stomachal disease

40. *rGyu-ma'i-nad* :   Diseases of small Intestine.

41. *long-nad* :   Diseases of Large Intestine

42. *pho-mtsan-nad*: Male genital diseases.

· 43. *mo-mtsan nad* : Female genital disease.

44. *sKad-'gags* :   Vocal obstruction.

45. *Yi-ga-'chus-pa* : Anorexia.

46. *sKom-dad* :   Excessive thirst..

47. *sKyigs-bu* :   Hiccough

48. *dbugs-mi-bde* : Respiratory disease.

49. *gLang-thabs* :   Sudden abdominal cramps.

50. *sRin-nad* :   Disorders caused by micro-organisms.

51. *sKyugs* :   Vomiting

52. *'Khru-nad*:   Diarrhoea.

53. *dri-ma-gags*:   Constipation

54. *gChin-'gags* : Dysuria

55. *gChin-sNyi* : Diabetes.

56. *tshad-'khru*: Dysentary.

57. *dreg* : Gout

58. *grum-bu* : Arthritis.

59. *Chu-ser-nad* : Excess serous fluid disease.

60. *rtsa-dkar-nad*: Nerve disorders.

61. *pags-nad* : Dermatological disorder.

62. *phran-bu'i-nad* : Miscellaneous minor disorders.

63. *'bras-nad*: The combination of blood, serous fluid and *rlung* disorders giving rise to internal and external maligant tumors.

64. *gZhang-'brum* : Haemorrhoids.

65. *me-dbal* : Erysipelas.

66. *Sur-ya* : Rounded red rash on the skin associated with sores on specific organs.

67. *rMen-bu'i-nad* : Lymphadenopathy

68. *rLig-rlug*s : Hydroceles.

69. *rKang-'bam* : Blood-*rlung*-combined disorder characterised with the swelling of legs.

70. *mtsan-bar-rdol* : Anal Fistula.

71. *byis-pa Nyer-spyod* : Regimens dealing with proper bringing up of the child in sound environment.

72. *byis-nad* : Paediatric disease.

73. *byis-pai-gdon* : Evil spirits causing Paediatric disorders.

74. *mo-nad-spyi*: General gynaecological disease.

75. *mo-nad-bye-brag*: Specific gynaecological disease.

76. *mo-nad-phal-ba* : Common gynaecological disease.

77. *'byung-po'i nad* : Disease caused by evil spirits

78. *sMyo* : Insanity

79. *brjed* : Amnesia.

80. *gZa'*: Epilepsy.

81. *klu-gdon nad* : Disorder caused by a particular evil spirit called klu or Naga a demi-god having the human head and the body of a serpent.

82. *rMa-spyi* : General wounds.

83. *mGo-rMa* : Head wounds.

84. *ske'i -rMa* : Cervical wounds.

85. *byang-khog-rMa* : Abdominal wounds.

86. *yan-lag-rMa* : Wounds of the extremities.

87. *sbyar-dug* : Compounded poison.

88. *gyur-dug* : Food poison.

89. *dNgos-dug* : Natural poison.

90. *bCud-len* : Rejuvenation

91. *ro-tsa* : Impotancy.

92. *bu-med-bstal* : Fertility.

IV *Phyima-rGyud*
(Last Tantra, 25 chapters).

1. *rtsa:* Sphygmology.

2. *Chu* : Urinalysis.

3. *Thang* : Decoction.

4. *phye-ma* : Powdered medicine.

5. *Ril-bu* : Pills.

6. *lde-gu* : Medicinal paste.

7. *sMan-mar* : Medicinal butter.

8. *Thal-sMan* : Medicinal ash.

9. *Khan-dra* : Concentrated decoction.

10. *sMan-chang* : Medicinal beverage.

11. *Rin-po-che* : Gem medicine.

12. *sNgo-sbyor* : Herbal compound.

13. *sNum-'chos* : The preliminary task of using oil for all the five works - emetics, purgatives etc.

14. *bshal* : Purgatives.

15. *sKugs* : Emeties.

16. *sNa-sMan* : Nasal medications.

17. *'jam-rtsi*: Mild suppository.

18. *ni-ru-ha* : Enema.

19. *rtsa-sbyong* :   Vessel cleansing techniques.

20. *gtar* :   Venesection.

21. *bsreg* : Moxibustion.

22. *dugs* : Compress therapy.

23. *Lums* :   Medicinal bath therapy.

24. *byug-pa* :   Massage therapy.

25. *thur-dpyad* :   Mild surgical methods.

BIBLIOGRAPHY

Barshi, Phuntsok Wangyal. *rTsa-chu'i Lhan-thabs mGus-pa'i mDzes-brgyan*. Dharamsala: Tibetan Medical Centre, 1979.

Choekyi Sangye (ed.). *gYu-thog sNying-thig gi Cho-ga'i Las-byang Cha-tsang*. Lhasa, Chag-po-ri, 1888.

Choekyi Thinley : *Zab-don Yid-bzin Nor-bu*. Originally written, ca. 15th century A.D. Reprinted Leh: Tashigang 1976.

Dharmo Menrampa, Lobsang Chodrak. *Dar-mo bKa' rGya-ma*. Leh: Tashigang, 1978.

_____ *gYu-thog Yon-tan mGon-po rNying-ma'i rNam-thar bKa'-rgya-ma*. Lhasa: Zhol Press, 1893.

-------------- *Man-dig gSer-rgyan*. Lhasa: Zhol Press, 1893.

-------------- *Phyi-rgyud Me-po'i Zhal-lung*. Lhasa: Zhol Press, 1893.

Deumar, Tenzin Phuntsok. *sMan-gyi Nus-pa Dri-med Shel-phreng*. Originally written in 1727. Reprinted Lhasa : Chag-pori Press, (?)

_____ *Lag-len gCes-bsdus*. Handwritten; date and place unknown.

_____ *dPyad-mchog gTar-kha'i gDams-pa*. Handwritten;

date and place unknown.

-------------- *Me-rtsa'i gDam-pa*. Handwritten; date and place unknown.

-------------- *Dug-nad gSo-ba'i Zin-tig*. Handwritten; date and place unknown.

-------------- *Ya-srin bCo-bsdus Don gSum-pa*. Handwritten; date and place unknown.

-------------- *rNgul-'byin gyi gDams-pa*. Handwritten; date and place unknown.

-------------- *Bi-sha bCos-pa'i Man-ngag*. Handwritten; date and place unknown.

-------------- *rMa bCos kyi bskor*. Handwritten; date and place unknown.

Drigung Chodrak Tinlay. *'Bam-bchos Tse-'zin Srog-skyobs*. Handwritten; ca. 17th century. A.D.

-------------- *'Bam-bchos Khag-gnyis*. Handwritten; ca. 18th century, A.D.

Gongmen Kunchog Phendar. *Nyam-yig brGya-rtsa*. Handwritten; Ladakh, ca. 16th century A.D.

Gongmen Kunchok Deleg. *gSo-rig dGos-pa Kun-'byung*. Leh: Tashigang, 1976.

Guruphel, Drungyid. *Si-tu'i sNan-rgyud*. Handwritten; ca. 18th century, A.D.

--------------- *dNgu-chu rTso-chen dang Rin-chen Ril-bu'i sByor-sde Zla-ba dBud-rtsi Thig-le*. Degye: Degye Press (?)

Gyatso, Desid Sangye. *Khog-dbug Drang-srong rGyas-pa'i dga' ston* Leh: Tashigang, 1973.

---------------- *rGyud-bzhi'i gSal-yed Vaidurga sNgon-po*. Lhasa: Zhol Press, 1893.

--------------- *Man-ngag Lhan-thabs*. Degye: Degye Press, 1734.

-------------- *Man-ngag Lhan-thabs kyi Lag-rgyun Zab-mo'i Zin-bris*. Leh: Tashigang, 1969.

Ju-Mipham, Jamyang Namgyal. *sMan-sbyor bDud-rtsi Thig-le*. Lhasa: Mentzi Khang Press.(?)

Kathog, Tsojed Dorje.*'Bam-bchos Lag-len sNying-po*. Handwritten; date and place unknown.

Kongpo Jangthod, Karma Rinchen. *Phan-bde 'Bum-phrag gyi sDe-mig*. Leh: Tashigang, 1969.

-------------- *Man-ngag Phan-bde 'Bum phrag*. Leh: Tashigang, 1969.

Karma, Dhondup Palden. *bsDus-spos 'Dod-dgu'i bang-mdzod Zhes sByor-dpe*. Degye: Degye Press.(?)

Kongtrul, Yontan Gyatso. *Zin-tig bDud-rtsi'i Thig-pa*. Lhasa: Mentzi Khang Press, 1916.

Khenrab , Norbu. *rGyud-bzhi'i Sa-bcad sTag-mo'i rNgam-thabs*. Sarnath: Tibetan Monastery Press, 1966.

------------ *rTsa-rgyud sDong-'grems gSo rig rGya-mtso'i sNying-po*. Sarnath: Tibetan Monastery Press, 1966.

------------ *bShad-rgyud sDong-'grems Zla-shel Nor-bu'i Me-long*. Sarnath: Tibtan Monastery Press, 1966.

------------ *Nyam-yig bsDus-'bring Rin-chen 'Phreng-ba*. Sarnath: Tibetan Monastery Press, 1966.

------------ *Phyi-rgyud bsDoms-tsigs*. Sarnath: Tibetan Monastery Press, 1966.

------------ *Lus-thig rGyas-pa Zla-ba Nor-bu'i Me long*. Sarnath: Tibetan Monastery Press, 1966.

------------ *rTsa-chu'i Lhan-thabs*. Sarnath: Tibetan Monastery Press, 1966.

------------ *gTar-rtsa'i bsDoms-tigs gZhon-nu'i Ngag-brgyan*. Sarnath: Tibetan Monastery Press, 1966.

------------ *Khrog-sman 'Khrung-dpe 'Dog-'jo'i Bum-bzang*.Sarnath: Tibetan Monastery Press, 1966.

------------ *sNgo-sman 'Khrung-dpe Ngo-btsar gSer gyi sNye-ma* Dharamsala: Tibetan Medical Centre, 1971.

------------ *sByor-dpe bDud-rtsi Bum-bzang.* Dharamsala: Tibetan Medical Centre, 1968.

Kyempa, Lhata Tsewang. *sKyem-pa'i gDam-ngag.* Handwritten; ca. 16th century A.D.

------------ *sLob-bu la gDam-pa'i Man-ngag.* Original, ca. 17th century A.D.

Ngawang Palsang. *Man-ngag Lhan-thabs kyi sDe-mig.* Degye: Degye Press, 1734.

Ngawang Rigned Gyatso. *rTsa-rgyud rNam-bshad Zhal-lung Don-gsal.* Leh: Tashigang, 1977.

Pael. *gSo-rig Man-ngag Phan-bde'i Yang-snying.* Leh: Tashigang 1977.

Karma Ngyelek Tenzin *gSo-rig bstan-bchos Phan-bde Zla-gser Ae.* Leh: Tashigang, 1973.

------------ *sMan-phyi'i Lhan-thabs Phan-bde dBang-mdzod Vam. Leh: Tashigang 1973.*

Sakya'i Jetsun Dragpa Gyaltsen. *gSo-dpyad rGyal-po'i dKor-mdzod.* Gangtok: Sir Tashi Namgyal Institute of Tibetology, 1966.

Sogpo Jampal Dorje. *Man-ngag Rinchen 'Byung-gnas.* Leh: Tashigang, 1974.

Sogpo Lungrik Tendar. *rGyud-bzhi brDa-don bKrol-ba rNam-*

rgyal A-ru-ra yi'Phreng-ba.

Rinchen Gyatso. *Lhan-thabs Zur-brgyan.* Handwritten, ca. 18th century A.D.

Tashi Palsang. *rTsa-phyi'i rGyud-'grel rGyud-don Rab-gsal.* Leh: Tashigang, 1977.

Tekhang, Jampa Thubwang. *Byi-pa Ner-spyond'Gro-phan sNying-nor.* Lhasa: Mentxi khang Press, 1916.

Terton Tagsham. *sTag-sham gTer-ma gNyan-bchos Ral-gri Phung-brgyan.* Handwritten; date and place unknown.

Urgan Tenzin. *Zin-tig mDzes-rgyan.* Leh: Tashigang, 1973.

Yuthog, Yontan Gonpo (Sarma). *bDud-rtzi sNying-po Yan-lag brGyad-pa gSang-ba Man-ngag gi rGyud* Lhasa: Zhol Press, 1893.

------------ *rGyud-bzhi dPe-rnying Man-phyi gNyis. Tsang* : Phuntsog Ling Press, 1460.

----------- *rGyud-gsum Tsa Shad Phyi.* Dharamsala: Tibetan Medical Centre, 1971.

----------- *Cha-lag bCho-brgyad.* Lhasa: Zhol Press, 1893.

Zurkhar, Lodroe Gyalpo. *rTsa-bshad'Grel-pa Me-po'i Zhal-lung.* Lhasa: Zhol Press, 1893.

----------- *Phi-rgyud rTsa-'grel Me-po'i Zhal-lung.* Lhasa: Zhol

Press, 1893.

----------- *dPon-tsang Phan-dar par bTang-ba'i Dri-ba rTsa-ta'i Khri-shing*. Handwritten; ca 15th century A.D.

----------- *rGyud-bzhi bKa-bstan gyi rNam-bzhag*. Handwritten; date and place unknown.

Zurkhar, Nyamnid Dorje. *Bye-ba Ring-srel gyi sDe'u-mig*. Handwritten; ca. 16th century A.D.

------------ *Zur-khyad Mu-zi'i gDam-pa*. Handwritten; ca. 15th century A.D.

------------ *Zur-khyad Norbu'i Phreng-ba*. Handwritten; ca. 15th century A.D.

----------- *Zur-khyad 'Brum-nag bChos*. Handwritten; ca. 15th century A.D.

------------ *Zur-khyad Mo-nad bChos*. Handwritten; ca. 15th century A.D.

------------ *Zur-khyad Dug-sbyor Rin-chen 'Phreng-ba*. Handwritten; ca. 15th century A.D.